Body Coverings

Scales

Cassie Mayer

www.heinemann.co.uk/library

Visit our website to find out more information about **Heinemann Library** books.

To order:

📞 Phone 44 (0) 1865 888066

📠 Send a fax to 44 (0) 1865 314091

💻 📖 Visit the Heinemann Bookshop at www.heinemann.co.uk/library to browse our catalogue and order online.

First published in Great Britain by Heinemann Library, Halley Court, Jordan Hill, Oxford OX2 8EJ, part of Harcourt Education. Heinemann is a registered trademark of Harcourt Education Ltd.

Editorial: Tracey Crawford, Cassie Mayer, Dan Nunn, and Sarah Chappelow
Design: Jo Hinton-Malivoire
Picture Research: Tracy Cummins
Production: Duncan Gilbert

Originated by Chroma Graphics (Overseas) Pte. Ltd
Printed and bound in China by South China Printing Company

10 digit ISBN 0 431 18279 5
13 digit ISBN 978 0 431 18279 7

10 09 08 07 06
10 9 8 7 6 5 4 3 2 1

British Library Cataloguing in Publication Data
Mayer, Cassie
Scales. – (Body coverings)
597.147

Acknowledgements

The publishers would like to thank the following for permission to reproduce photographs:

Alamy p. **22** (eagle, Nature Picture Library/Jeff Foott); Corbis pp. **7** and **8** (Joe McDonald), **9** and **10** (scales, Clouds Hill Imaging Ltd.), **10** (shark, Tim Davis), **11** and **12** (Nigel J. Dennis/Gallo Images), **13** (microscopic scales, George D. Lepp and butterfly, Ralph A. Clevenger), **20** (Kevin Dodge); Getty Images pp. **6** (Allofs), **14** (Bumgarner), **15** (Rotman), **16** (Wolcott Henry III), **17** (Wolfe), **18** (Wolfe), **23** (Wolfe); Getty Images/Digital Vision pp. **4** (kingfisher, cheetah, and rhino); Getty Images/PhotoDisc p. **4** (snail), **5**, **23**; Nature Picture Library p. **22** (turtle, Jeff Rotman); NHPA p. **22** (shark, Doug Perrine).

Cover image of scales reproduced with permission of Strand/Getty Images. Back cover image of snake scales reproduced with permission of Joe McDonald/Corbis.

Special thanks to the Smithsonian Institution and Alfonso Alonso, Gary E. Davis, Helen Ghiradella, Olivier S.G. Pauwels, and Robert Robbins for their help with this project.

Every effort has been made to contact copyright holders of any material reproduced in this book. Any omissions will be rectified in subsequent printings if notice is given to the publishers.

The paper used to print this book comes from sustainable resources.

Contents

All animals have body coverings.
Look at these body coverings.

feathers

skin
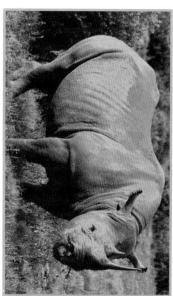

fur

shell

scales

This animal has scales.
Scales are a body covering too.

There are different types of scales.

Scales can be smooth.
What animal is this?

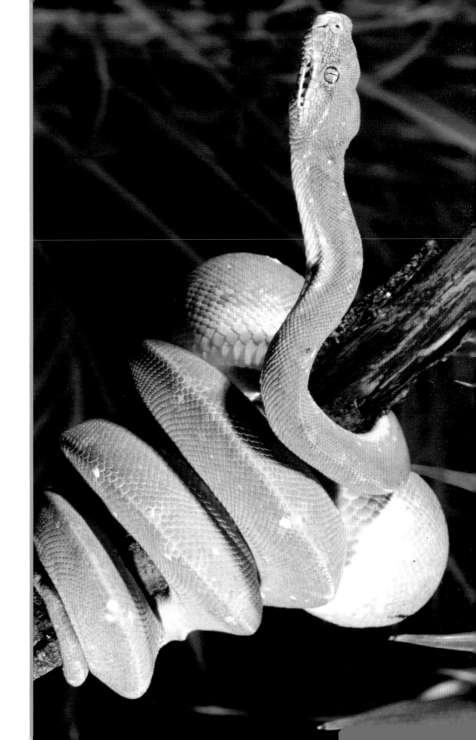

This animal is a snake.
Its scales help it to move.

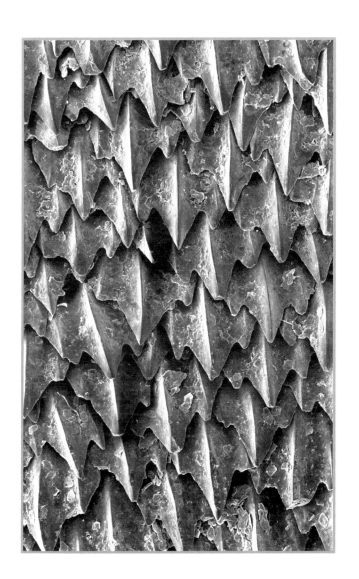

Scales can be rough.
What animal is this?

This animal is a shark.
Its scales are very sharp.

Scales can be big.
What animal is this?

This animal is a pangolin.
Its scales are as big as your hand.

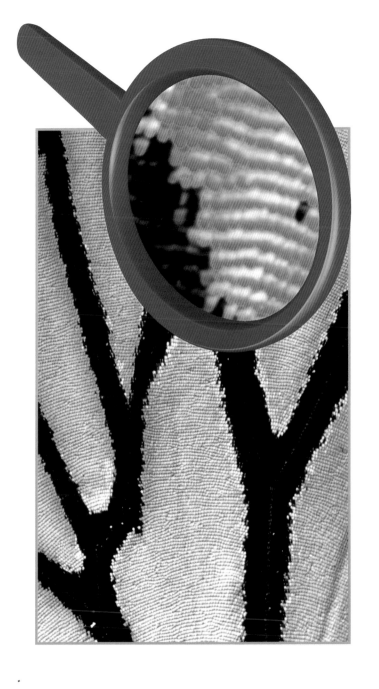

Scales can be small.
What animal is this?

This animal is a fish.

Its bright scales say "Danger!".

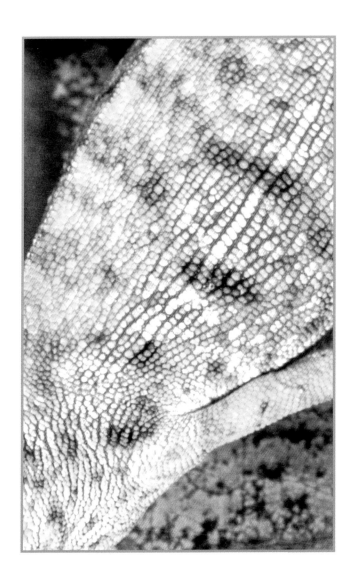

Scales can have patterns.
What animal is this?

This animal is a lizard.
Its scales help it to hide.

Do you have scales?

No! You do not have scales!
You have skin.

Scales quiz

(answers on page 24)

1. I swim in the sea.
   I have sharp scales.
   I have big teeth.
   What am I?

2. I can fly.
   I like flowers.
   My scales are too small to see.
   What am I?

Fun scale facts

Bald eagles have scales on their feet.

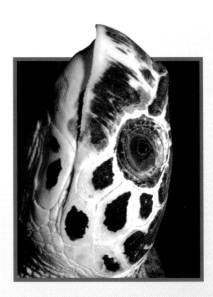

Turtles have a beak. Their beak is a scale.

Shark teeth are a type of scale.

Picture glossary

pattern an arrangement of markings. Patterns on scales help animals to hide.

scale a type of body covering

Index

Notes to parents and teachers

Before reading

Talk about how animals have different body coverings – fur, feathers, shells, scales, and skin. Talk about the different kinds of scales – some scales are smooth (snake), some scales are sharp (shark), some scales are large (pangolin), and some scales are tiny (butterfly). Talk about how fur helps animals to keep warm and protects them from enemies.

After reading

Collect examples of different body coverings – fun fur, feathers, shells. (Make scales by drawing scales on to cardboard and scoring the lines). Encourage children to describe the different textures and colours. Put the body coverings in a "feely box" and challenge children to identify them. Cut out pictures of animals and help children to sort them into the different body coverings. Making a snake skin: Rub green, brown, and red crayons on long strips of paper with a bicycle tyre underneath then cut into snake shapes. Talk about the scaly pattern.

Answers to quiz: 1. I am a shark. 2. I am a butterfly.

Titles in the *Body Coverings* series include:

Hardback 0 431 18281 7

Hardback 0 431 18280 9

Hardback 0 431 18279 5

Hardback 0 431 18278 7

Hardback 0 431 18282 5

Find out about other titles from Heinemann Library on our website www.heinemann.co.uk/library